MW01624714

ISBN 0-9668182-0-2
Library of Congress Number 2001132843

Published by
ARDMORE PUBLISHING COMPANY
Atlanta, Georgia

second printing

Lest you forget

Violet Gray Witherspoon

The Poems

of

Violet Witherspoon

In this book are 33 poems written by a woman who died in 1954. She was 81 years old.

Her name was Violet Gray Witherspoon, and she lived her entire life in Macon, Georgia.

These poems tell the story of her long relationship with a man named John Chambers who also lived in Macon and who died there in 1926. He was a newspaperman and at one time an editor of the Macon *Evening News*, which later became the Macon *News* and was published into the 1990s.

Violet Witherspoon was not a prolific writer. Mostly her work included poems, stories, and a sporadic journal of isolated events she found interesting.

Beyond that, she kept a not unusual amount of letters and notes, including many from John as well as her own letters to John, which he had apparently returned to her at some point, very likely to ensure privacy.

All put together, their correspondence suggests the two became sweethearts in the late 1880s when Violet was a college student in Macon but that in 1893 her attention was taken by an attorney named Lamar Witherspoon, a lecturer at the college, whom she married the next year.

A year later, John married Agatha Shepherd, a young woman from Sandersville, a little town sixty miles east of Macon.

Neither marriage was long lasting.

Lamar died in 1900 of pleurisy, leaving Violet with one daughter, Mae.

John and Agatha had two children who both died that same year of scarlet fever. Shortly afterwards, Agatha moved back to her family's home in Sandersville and stayed there almost a recluse until her death in November 1912. It was said she suffered from a weakened heart brought on by the loss of the two infants.

After Lamar's death and after Agatha left Macon, Violet and John came together again, though with John still bound to the relationship with his wife, they were forced to maintain a façade of friendship, which they continued even after Agatha died.

The poems here are dated from 1902 to 1939. Most are addressed directly to John.

How a relationship of the depth the poems indicate endured privately for more than twenty years in a town as small as Macon, which at the turn of the century had a population of only 23,000, is difficult to imagine.

Equally perplexing is why Violet and John did not marry after Agatha's death.

But those were proper Victorian times, and the South has always been proper.

For whatever reasons, Violet Witherspoon and John Chambers have kept their secret for almost a century. These are her poems.

I

What calls to me,
  draws me here?
Perhaps your smile,
Perhaps my tears that fell upon our parting.
But no; 'tis more.
'Tis the things never noticed,
Or if noticed,
Things you'd doubtless change:
The sweetness of the heart
  that a man would disdain,
The absence of words
  when others would orate,
The hand yet open
  when my own fails to meet the touch,
The gentle song
  learned from a mother's love.
These dear things
Above all those cheered by the crowd
Who know neither ecstasy nor mercy of affection,
These things summon me,
Speak to me,
Draw me here to you.

January 3, 1902

II

The heart is joyful with fear,
Glad and grave,
Timorous, brave, and all contradictory things
That are when spirit demurs, soul sings,
  and one is near.
Should words be given breath,
Shall the same see ashen death
  in silence?
Do not look upon my fingers
  shivering like grasses in the wind;
They betray the heart and all its prisoned thoughts within.
Only hear the words.
To cherish or to spurn, they are given.
Say nothing in return.

June 6, 1902

III

When I speak of love, this will it mean:
I will touch your face in happiness
    all the time of my living
    and all the time of yours.
I will give you what goodness my soul can find,
    what honor, respect, what admiration.
I will live inside, indeed under your being.

When I speak of love,
    I will sing the songs of ages.
I will give you my gold, my house,
    all that I am worth.
I will open to you the doors of my dreams.

Accept these not as mine
    but as what you give to me.
These strange gifts I will offer
    when I speak of love.

November 12, 1902

IV

No debt is owed a smile, however warm,
That brightened hearthstone cold on gray-branched day,
Nor dearness of an eye that shone with special charm
And lighted lowest clouds along their way.
For spoken kindness let no payment pass,
Though in truth such never fell unheard,
Nor yet for look, nor dress, nor studied stance
Seen loudly clothed in pale and dying word.
Only a sightless scene deserves the fee:
'Twas but a hand laid lightly o'er my own,
A momentary mime, mute reverie,
For hands sing songs with words to lips unknown.
Unseen by thee who played the mummer's part,
In recompense for hand, I gave my heart.

January 3, 1905

Lamar Witherspoon

whom Violet married in 1894

V

More shall never come;
  no fuller breath,
  no brighter sight,
  no sweeter song
Shall travel here
  than thee
Who brings to me, Dear Spirit,
Blooms of every ecstasy.
Thou art my closest thought
  from years ago to now
  and yet to days unborn.
Thou art my love.
In thee do I live on.

December 6, 1906

VI

To gather up the winds and waters of the world
   with open-fingered hands,
To vision into blackness of the night
   with sightless eyes,
To spin my being into timeless, airless space
   for passion's sake:
Such is the longing for my Distant Spirit,
   harvester of my past,
   taker of tomorrow's dreams,
   my untouched phantom
   whose half-illumined visage, like the moon,
   circles 'round me slowly,
   deepening purple shadows,
   weaving shrouds to wrap my soul.

February 2, 1907

VII

A Little Song

Do I love you?
'Deed I do.
Sure as jonquils come rushing through the ground
  on a February morning,
Sure as jaybirds call a rainstorm
  when clouds hang heavy overhead,
Sure as summer's sun turns the earth deep red
  and bleaches skies pale blue,
Sure as the land wakes up cold and still
  before the day's first footsteps break the frost,
Sure as all things ought to live
  and all living things have to die,
I love you.
'Deed I do.

May 26, 1907

VIII

Through softest thoughts
She gazed at songs and visions blurred by long ago.
She reminisced the future with the past.
"Thus shall our lives be spent,"
spoke the lady of the dream.
"I with thee through winters frozen,
in summers abloom with life;
I with thee,
my hand to touch thy hand with open palm,
my lips to kiss the sadness of thy thoughts,
my eyes to see thy joys;
I with thee,
my being to fly with thy being
beyond our seeing and our hearing
to points in darkness our thinking cannot know."
The Spirit who saw her speak
Smiled into the weeping candles
This night and many nights to come.
His fate it was to see her times again,
Her words floating above more candles
Lighting flickers of remembrance.
But the lady, who recalls him in her yesterdays,
Sees now what he cannot:
the dance beneath the hour glass,
the chiming of the clock.
She knows that sadness fosters bliss
and gladness deep despair
For one who wanders through the doors of time
Searching for the Spirit traveling with her
Who hears her only in the deepest dreams
of what has gone before.

November 4, 1907

St. Paul's Episcopal Church in Macon
where Violet and Lamar were married

IX

I remember you from places I cannot name,
But I remember you, Beloved.
As then, today you are the same –
  the Spirit who fain will come to earth and to me.

Tarry here awhile.
Let the rememberings and today
  become what used to be reality.
And I shall love this moment,
And I shall wait through one more set of years
  or two or three
Till our lives converge in single living,
Till you are one in soul and time with me.

August 27, 1909

X

Not in this autumn do you walk my way,
Not in these dwindling, dying days,
This season of artificial hope, of lower evening star.
No figure approaches from afar.

Other Octobers I have stood long where the roads cross,
Watching colors die on the ground,
Feeling the near frost,
Mourning decrescendos of summer's sounds.

Twilight drops; the road darkens and is cold.
Shadows fall long-fingered, old.
Northward flies a crow bearding winter's pain.
No one travels here this autumn, once again.

October 30, 1909

XI

’Tis best, ’tis said,
    to keep one’s heart;
’Tis safer there,
    ’tis said.
Yet what custodian,
    awakening,
Has pondered the wardenship
And longed to lie abed?

May 8, 1910

XII

My lost saints journey home
To a throne reverenced years ago,
A sovereign place, solid, gold,
Unshakable as stone
Where once they spoke on every thought and word.
Folly warred with them, and winning, turned them out,
    some in languor,
    some in scorn.
Living now reclaims them one by one.
On gentle feet my lost saints journey home.

July 13, 1911

XIII

Eleven years again I have known you –
  two for learning,
  two more for closeness;
  the remainder I have loved you.

Eleven springs have passed to summers,
  have burned to the glory of autumns.

Now before the light of winter's fire
  I ponder all our seasons,
  dreaming, doubting, dreading
  what more are ours to come.

January 18, 1912

Agatha Shepherd

shortly after her marriage to John Chambers

XIV

Secrets there are within my soul,
Secrets that breathe only in the lightest moments
When all about is sombre, safe, and even cold.
'Tis then they soar to heights unfathomed.
In private moments my secrets live a life
  that never faces death from disappointment,
A life that flies into a sky of stars
  years of lives away.
Free have been my secrets,
Free to dream, to dip, to soar where e're they may.
Whst! A word calls them to task.
How dreadful that my secrets cannot last!

December 7, 1912

XV

When death reels in life's spool of silken twine,
When suns are dark, yet lamps are lit no more,
When past in future archives' dust is stored,
Then shall our two souls touch in void of time.
Immortal thoughts of mortals, lost in sighs,
Sleep sweetly, ringed in orbs of candle gold;
Youth's fairest hand embraces hands grown cold;
Nine winged angels trumpet death shall die.
When breaks that morn of never-counted days,
When bramble thorn adorn our separate graves,
I'll waken from a dreamless, ancient nap
And searching, find thine earthen door and rap
Lightly, then with ghostly kiss wake thee.
Good Spirit, we shall share Forever's eve.

February 10, 1913

XVI

Now twelve years have I known
    all the faces that emotion can portray.
Now twelve years have I known
    the living revenant
    raging through my soul and breathing life.
Now twelve years have I known
    the madness of delight
    tempered by the neutrality of separateness.
My hand touches thy impermanent spirit,
My fingers pass over, around,
Circumscribe thy essence with a thousand threads
Yet restricting none but me.
Now twelve years have I known
    the glibness of talk,
    gaity and despair,
    frenzy, rapture, agony, bliss,
What all is love, what all is words,
What all of this is purely mine
And what is thee.

September 21, 1913

Agatha's family home in Sandersville, Georgia.
Agatha died here in 1912. The house burned in the 1950s.

XVII

Before this time of measured hour,
In prayers that later fled to their tomorrows' reveries,
In long agos, I knew that one would come to one
    who gazed far into yesterdays
    searching for the stranger
            clothed in memories ne'er expressed.
O Beloved Spirit,
Thy head rests now upon my breast!

March 10, 1914

XVIII

The Seduction

The phantom made his gracious bow by night,
Smiling smiles that lit a light
Within me; my thoughts flew flights
I never dreamed existed till that sight.

His voice spoke in monotone,
And on and on it droned and droned
About things I'd never cared to know
But thrilled me to the bone.

In retrospect, I think I tried
For wit and charm and thus belied
The shortened breath I sought to hide
Behind demeanor's downhill slide.

But comes a point, early or late,
That every lady knows
(or prays to know if such is not her fate)
When niceties and manners count for naught,
And all she wants to see is havoc being wrought.

In heart of hearts I somehow knew
That my queer thoughts were his thoughts too,
That his calm gaze but veiled the truth,
That he caused this commotion's brew.

He took my hand, and every trace
Of decency and ladyhood to the doorway raced.
I only hoped he wouldn't hear the quickened pace
Of pulse or see what lay behind my face.

The phantom's vision touched my dress
Such that I could only guess
His mischief: "Will you be my guest
And dance here in the dark with me?"
I said yes.

Around the room in waltz and spin
We dipped and whirled around again,
And care went whistling down the wind.
We danced till dawn on wings of sin.

December 30, 1914

XIX

My private sadness
   knocks upon the door,
And at no answer
   walks to the house's side
   to peer through the panes.
Should no one come there still,
   shouts then my sadness loud
   toward all the other rooftops,
   begging a spot to bide awhile.

Shh! Shh!! The neighbors will hear
                              this defiling of the place
   and tiptoe here some night whilst I sleep
   to burn the house down
   for fear some creature as you
   might creep beyond these bounds
   to their own lives.

Come in, dear Sadness.
Leave the neighbors to their safety and chagrin.
Laugh, if you must,
   as I muse the deadly moments of the past
   and vision you, less painful,
As a sort of friend.

January 3, 1915

The house in Macon where Violet lived from the early 1900s until her death

XX

Camelot dies,
    perhaps is dead.
Once rose gold in evening's light,
Camelot's stones lie broken, gray with ash.
Its music sings no songs.

I think it was a fire that consumed Camelot.
I think it was a fire
    that would not stay just warm within the walls
But had to roar out till the castle
    could hold it back no more.

No matter.
Camelot, dead, remains a lovely memory.
Sweet summer's sleep wakes now to morn.

April 11, 1915

XXI

When you go,
Make the leaving swift.
Cut the ties cleanly
As if you would forget the past.

Let rain wash out your footsteps;
Let sun claim old bones
And bleach them chalky white.
Do not dally into the new life.

After, if tomorrow's morning dims,
If a winter's gust creeps through cracks in the door,
Heaps snow by the porch,
Creaks the floorboards within,
Remember then
The time when phantoms of a firesong
Warmed hearth and hand and face,
Lighted care,
Calmed the pace of living,

Remember too
The swelling of the buds,
The waiting for blossoms set to burst,
First signs of summer that almost came.

In that winter
This musing shall remain:
Two spirits once shared a day
That ended swiftly
But did not fade away.

August 25, 1915

XXII

If I could speak the thoughts that thrash
    beneath my voice
    like wild birds frantic to escape the cage,

If I could sing the songs that lift me
    off my feet sometimes
    on puffs of air,

If I could write the words that swing around my head
    on long and unconnected strings

Or paint the dreams that race across my nights
    and disappear,

You would know what overtakes me
    tip to toe,
    catches my breath,
    quickens my fire,
    fills my fingers with a passion I cannot express
When you are near.

May 7, 1919

XXIII

Passion fumes from your soul
  absorbing into my own.
Passion shrieks from your soft voice
  reverberating through my person's sounds.
Your fire brightens my seeing.
Your music in time, in rhyme
  dances through my thoughts,
  spins my dreams to clarity.
You are the Spirit who draws my breathing
  inward,
  outward,
  animating the fantasy that keeps my life living
  and sweetening the lips of death
  with the songs of all my years' histories.
You are my rhythm, my cadence,
  the breathless swelling of my breast
  that opens my windows to the oneness of ecstasy,
For it is you who owns my love.

May 10, 1920

XXIV

The traveler walks through far-off regions,
    witnesses unimagined visions,
    answers the voices of strangers.
The traveler crosses lines and bounds
    farther than maps can chart,
    wakes and sleeps to days born and dying
    in hours ajar to the chime of my clock.

Asleep against an unremarkèd night,
    deaf to foreign phrases,
    unsighted to the measures of the miles,
A house awaits a knock upon its solitary door.
The traveler pauses at the window,
    thence to the fire within,
    only to turn his thinking on the skirt of a moment
    to times and distances neither house nor occupant shall see.

Thus does the journey begin anew.
Yet in ending is the destination ever the same:
    to the house, to the tenebrous night,
    to the unreckoned hours, and to me.

March 21, 1921

XXV

Remembrance

Across the room appeared a face, older now,
But whose smile time never touched.
And in the quieter eyes I thought to see again
The glimmer that waited there once for me
    and died by my hand.

Thirty years have lived since that passing,
Yet thirty years do not erase regret
Or silence memories of the smile
Or cause my own eyes to glimmer less
For the face across the room.

April 13, 1923

Wesleyan College, where Violet was a student and Lamar Witherspoon served as a lecturer. Above is the original building,

which was built in 1836. The photo on this page is the same building after it was renovated to the Victorian style in 1881.

XXVI

Death wind blew forth from summer,
A night's wind of stars obscured,
    breathing the curse of March.

Afloat upon the air, cavern-sounding spirits
Sang cold songs, awakened from a sleep in a hollow hall.

In long procession of muffled steps,
The winds of sin paraded around my life
Mumbling chants my soul has ever feared:
    "Time is passed.
    No mercy waits for those who ask too much of life.
    No heaven shall receive thee.
    The rusty doors of light to thee are closed."

Round and round,
    in spirals growing wider, growing small,
The wind sucked up my breath,
Spewing forth my being and all my thoughts
    for keeping life alive,
Leaving only sorrow there behind
    to hear the story of the time
That lived before the wind of summer
Blowing from another part of year.

May 28, 1923

XXVII

Fear not the night,
Dread not the dark
Whose pall spreads o'er thy sight,
Whose fingers mark thy forehead
  in frozen runic write.
'Tis but the morning of an unremembered life.

When the blackened moment comes,
When the frightful fear appears,
Whether there or here,
Look then for me
Who draws thy final breath away,
Who grasps thy marble hand,
Who leads thee to the softness
  of a place I made for thee
In the long-forgotten day
  we lived before our current light,
When we waited for the ending of a future
  that is now.

July 8, 1924

XXVIII

August 1892

More years than I had then lived
  have passed after that August.
More years have laid mild hands
  against my cheek and my eyes
  and touched the tone of your hair,
  though in kindness
  they never altered your smile.

The late day nods; its chin droops
  in an old man's doze;
  it mulls our callow talk of this tomorrow.

At summer's close,
I grieve the once bright colors
  faded now to neutral shades
And rue the abandonment of our sweet August days.

August 29, 1924

XXIX

What comes of love?
Do passing hours soften corners
In such a way that what then was love
Becomes now the face of God
Yet unrecognized?

Or does emotion fade,
Having lived its time, and knowing that,
Gather up its wisdom to pursue another route?

Or does a darkness fall,
And snatching passion in its hands,
Consign it to sweet memory?

Hold what has lived a worthy life,
For love is an elder thing
Sitting in the umbra of its years.
Reverence the deeds it has accomplished;
Cherish its tears.
Carry it to the morning of the next time of living.
Then look into the eyes of your treasure:
My soul appears.

May 15, 1925

XXX

Remember me
Who travels toward another life.
When comes that moment new,
Remember me.
My hands reach now from night
  lit not to you;
My ghost shouts silent words;
My eyes weep dry tears.
To you, for you, I will return.
Then, my closest soul,
Remember me.
Oh, remember me!

November 28, 1925

XXXI

Chill blew October's piercing breath at morn
Fading frosty stars that broke through night's clear sky.
'Twas the prelude to the fugue, the ever-waiting arms
That would embrace us in the winter of our time.
Brown-gold mellowed leaves soon to die
Consumed by flames of counterfeited life
Flew by on windy swirls in throes of death,
The grande waltz before the clock should strike.
As latened days of burnished beauty passed
From brightness into winter's graying,
Then did I and you together lift the mask
Of summer from the face of truth. We knew
That when there comes an autumn gloriously gold,
Singing sweet tunes and praying summer's smile,
Color soon shall pale in snowy cold
And memory freeze in winter's icy while.

November 9, 1928

XXXII

When our wanderings are finished,
   the ink blotted on the paper,
   the pages closed in the cupboard
   and sepiaed about the edges,
When the clever words have been honed to sharpest wit,
   the philosophies conferenced too many times,
Then an easeful chair and a quiet fire
   will bring forth sweet nods,
   clouding the days when every moment had purpose,
   when every spirit stood ready to burst forth laughter
                                                   and new desire.

There I shall remember love's passion
   and in so doing, wish away the sadness
   that falls damp like a gray fog
   over those who have experienced fancy and obsession
   but never love's drowsiness.

I shall whisper your name into the flame's glow:
   "Good Spirit! do you hear?"
The whisper will travel, as we did,
   farther than to the fingertips of the stars
   to touch your deep sleep.
In our dreams and near dreams, we shall grieve the blindness
   that hid from our vision love's old chairs,
   low fires in little parlors,
   reposeful foreheads,
   and death.

January 4, 1933

Violet as an old woman.
Taken in Macon in the 1940s.

XXXIII

Lest You Forget

You who happen upon us
    after our time has passed to dust,
    transforming our physical selves to oneness with the earth,
Should you, brushing aside the leaves
    that blanket our separate graves
    and reading words of letters soft now with age,
    think us but citizens of a distant day,
Reach to your faintest memories:
Might it be your hand that wrote these lines,
    your eyes that brimmed with tears at the leaving?
We two shall search for other homes.
Look closely at the stones.
They count our unlived moments;
They chronicle your days now gone.

February 5, 1939

John Chambers

The Photographs

The photos on the pages facing poems *IV*, *IX*, *XIV*, *XXXII*, and *XXXIII* and the photo of Wesleyan College after its Victorian renovation are courtesy of the Middle Georgia Archives of the Washington Memorial Library in Macon, Georgia.

The photo facing poem *XVII* is courtesy of James Buck of Lovejoy, Georgia.

The photo facing poem *XIX* is courtesy of Katy Sheridan of Macon, Georgia.

The photo of the original building of Wesleyan College is courtesy of Wesleyan College Archives, Macon, Georgia.

And the frontispiece is courtesy of Patsy Eaves Long of Atlanta, Georgia.